Navigating Education's
UNCHARTED
TERRITORY

A Move From Transactional to
Transformational Learning

Denice Dixon

Library of Congress Cataloging – in-
Publication Data has been applied for.

Paperback ~ 979-8-9894778-6-9
Kindle ~ 979-8-9894778-5-2

PRINTED IN THE UNITED STATES OF AMERICA.

FIRST EDITION

Table of Contents

Introduction

ey There! Thank you so much for purchasing this book. I know the climate of educational institutions have been under attack lately, but as a former elementary school teacher, I would like to introduce to you a new concept of education that will help correct our broken education system. Now, please know that this is not just another memoir or self-help book trying to persuade you to change your ideals of education and how or what should be taught in our classrooms. Although my journey as a teacher was rewarding, it was also met with adversity that changed the way I looked at education thereafter. This change happened in the year when one of my six-year-old students brought a gun to school and pulled it out in my classroom. As my emotions grew, the educator in me collided with the activist I didn't know existed within. However, when the justice I was looking for wasn't delivered, it was glaringly clear that our education system and the desire to protect a school's image were the highest factors in the scenario.

We overlooked the most critical aspect of education: the emotional and psychological needs of each child and staff. Due to their lack of accountability, I left my position in that school and ventured into the world of teacherpreneurship – a term that encapsulates the spirit of a teacher and the innovation of an entrepreneur. This book details this journey, from the traumatic experiences in a classroom to the student-centered learning program established to make learning fun and meaningful for students, with a bigger vision to revolutionize learning for all students.

As I write this book, I reflect on the recent challenge I encountered – being one of only six black educators among a group of 300. Now, I stand on the brink of another challenge: bringing together the right individuals to engage in crucial conversations about reshaping education and the necessity to do that as a collective. One of my goals for this book is to guide entrepreneurs, especially from black and brown communities, to shift from a mindset of self-interest to one of collective empowerment and to offer a beacon to educators forging new schools, lighting their way to triumph.

If you have ever been employed with the public education system, you have seen students constantly fall behind academically, being bullied, the social and emotional crisis that students are in, the disconnect between administrators and teachers, the disconnect between teachers and parents, and the broken system that you once believed could make a difference in the life of a child. In " Navigating Education's Unchartered Territories," you will get a chance to dream beyond the classroom with this new innovative model that is proving to be effective in the lives of children. You will read firsthand experiences with practical insights and a guide offering a new perspective on education.

Welcome to the story of one woman's transformation to teach students to achieve academic success through holistic global individual educational experiences that ultimately lead them to achieve their dreams. By introducing students to things happening around the world, they are better prepared to face today's challenges and work in tomorrow's economy.

Prelude

Over the past two centuries, schooling has undergone a profound transformation, evolving from the one-room schoolhouses of the 19th century that served small, rural populations to the expansive, tiered systems of the modern era. As industrialization surged, the demand for a more educated workforce led to compulsory education laws, giving rise to the public school system in the late 19th and early 20th centuries. The 20th century saw further democratization of education, with efforts to make schooling more inclusive and equitable. There were increased efforts towards educational equality, with federal acts such as the Civil Rights Act of 1964 and the Elementary and Secondary Education Act of 1965. These laws aimed to protect students from discrimination and to provide equal opportunities in education. Despite these efforts, disparities in educational resources, quality, and outcomes persisted due to systemic racism and socioeconomic factors.

In recent decades, there has been a push for educational reforms to address these disparities, including the introduction of charter schools, voucher programs, and other school choice options that some in the Black community have embraced to obtain a better education for their children. Today, the educational landscape for Black students is marked by ongoing challenges and the continued fight for equity and access to quality education. Now, in the 21st century, the digital revolution is reshaping education again, allowing for personalized learning experiences and the rise of alternatives like microschools, which reflect a return to the intimate learning environments of the past, albeit enhanced by technology and modern pedagogical insights. Could microschools be the solution to a two-century-old issue?

In the evolving landscape of education, microschools stand out as a beacon of innovation, offering a small-scale, highly personalized approach to learning. These intimate settings cater to the unique needs of each student, stepping away from the one-size-fits-all curriculum of traditional schools. Embracing the ethos of the one-room schoolhouse, microschools serve mixed-age groups, often with 50 students or less, and integrate the latest technology to tailor the educational experience. Microschools are flexible not just in their curriculum but also in their structure. Parents can opt for schedules that deviate from the conventional school day, choosing part-time or condensed hours that better fit their child's learning pace and their family's lifestyle. This model's versatility is a response to a critical need for adaptability highlighted by the pandemic, as families sought continuity in their children's education amidst widespread school closures.

Despite their promise and the growing interest from communities, there's a noticeable gap in leadership diversity within the microschool movement. As the sector expands, it's clear that while students of varied backgrounds are finding a home in these innovative environments, the representation of Black leaders at the helm remains low. Despite the high engagement of Black families, with 9%

of Black parents reporting their children's participation in microschools and a notable 49% expressing a desire to learn more, only 12.9% of current microschool leaders are Black. It's crucial for the future of microschools that leaders reflect the communities they serve, bringing a wealth of perspectives to the forefront of educational reform. This ensures that the revolutionary potential of microschools is fully realized, providing an inclusive, equitable, and enriching educational experience for all children. With the right support and encouragement, there is a significant opportunity for Black educators and entrepreneurs to step into leadership roles and shape the future of microschooling, ensuring that this innovative model benefits a diverse array of learners.

Chapter 1:
A Vision Takes Root

I knew I wanted to be a teacher from the time I was in 2nd grade. Many people change their ideas about what they want to be when they grow up, so they go off to college and try several different majors. But that's not my story. Teaching is what I knew that I would always do. As a child, my play involved creating lesson plans for stuffed animals. I found joy in helping siblings and friends with homework. I always valued education because my parents went out of their way to ensure I attended the best schools. I loved school, and my teachers recognized and nurtured my potential. My parents, until this day, joke about how I would cry if I had to miss a day of school because I was sick. When people asked me for help, I found satisfaction in the lightbulb moments they would experience. As I grew, this intrinsic drive to teach would grow with me. I went off to college, got my teaching credentials, and accepted a job offer doing the work I always dreamed of. I aspired to be a great teacher, then principalship, and then off to the collegiate level or the board of education, but as you will read, this roadmap shifts dramatically.

I am sitting in the car with my family on a Sunday morning, headed to church. Al Sharpton is on the radio, and he has just done an interview about those who are incarcerated and then released from prison with no education or skills to be a productive citizen. During his talk, I began typing notes into my phone, not about what he was saying but what was being revealed to me. It was the idea of me creating an alternative school that was in partnership with the juvenile jail system to have juveniles released to me upon their exit so that they could work on their GED and vocational skills. It would cater to the specific needs of each student and provide a caring and collaborative environment so that they would have a better chance at turning their life around and being productive citizens.

I sat in church just pondering what had just been revealed to me, and I couldn't see a way forward because my life goal was to teach, be a principal, and end my career as a professor. I did not want to start a school. I didn't know the least bit about owning a business. So, I took matters into my own hands and applied to be a teacher in the juvenile jail system. Long story short, I got hired but did not accept the position because of the many risks that came with it. The cons outweighed the pros, and I saw more barriers to achieving my goals than opportunities. And so, I continued working in the school system but I never lost sight of that day. It was clear to me that there had to be a way to keep our students engaged in school so that they did not have idle time to get into unnecessary trouble.

The school pipeline to prison data weighed heavily on me. These students are funneled out of public schools and into the juvenile justice system. Many of these children have learning disabilities or underachievement in school, histories of poverty, and/or neglect and would benefit from additional educational and holistic services. Instead, they are isolated, punished, and pushed out. For many of these students, their reading abilities were almost non-existent. I wanted to be a part of the team that would create this change, but I never thought it would unfold and flourish into the educational infrastructure that I have been able to create and that I want you to be able to create as well.

When the opportunity presented itself to be an effective teacher, like turning around a situation where educational progression was at a loss for a minority community, I raised my hand to participate. I was coming from another public school where I was doing phenomenal work, but it wasn't appreciated, and the school was filled with drama and chaos, none of which I signed up for. So, my first year at the charter school was inspiring and hopeful. I felt like we had all the right people in place to see the light at the end of the tunnel. My team of special education teachers and the co-teachers whose classrooms we pushed into were all on the same page in regard to what worked best for students. Our students were making strides and achieving big gains. I loved being able to have the autonomy and support to do what was best for students and to meet them at their point of need. I even signed up to work for the school's summer program that year because many of the students that we served were likely to show regression over the course of two months without our continued work to meet educational goals for them.

Going into year two, many teachers left the school; we had a lot of administrative changes, teachers changing grade levels, new rules, routines, and new curriculums. I am not against change within an organization. Change is often needed for growth. Change is expected when the ideas we have are not as effective as we thought they would be; however, change should not be experimental. This is a perspective that while change is often implemented with a desire for a specific outcome, an experiment is conducted with an openness to any number of possible results. This phase of the school was more experimental, and everyone hoped for the best. I had anxiety about this phase because our black students are in dire need of progressive education, and there was no time for "any number of possible results." We had the data from year one, and that data should have driven the changes for the next school year.

This crisis unfolded during my second year in a charter system tasked with revitalizing underperforming schools. I was so excited when I heard about this work to be change-makers in education that would be happening in our local school system. What began as an enthusiastic commitment to what I thought was educational reform quickly evolved into a discouraging scene of teacher burnout, administrative changes, and a growing disconnect between the school's mission and its execution.

As year two took off, I was already feeling like many teachers were... burned out! The year started at such a fast pace, and we did everything we could to make sure learning was happening. However, we were met with resistance from the administration, curriculum restraints, time restraints, politics of education, parents blaming us as the teacher instead of holding their child accountable, work-life balance, and the list goes on and on. I felt all of these pressures but very heavily the pressure of politics taking over education and favoritism between administration and staff. It is not a good feeling when the teacher next door gets more attention and recognition from the administration because they talk a little louder or spend more time in the office in the morning. To me, these are the teachers looking to get leveled up not by their work with children but by their way with words. As the saying goes, action speaks louder than words, and I am confident that no action was taking place in some of these classrooms, but somehow, their way with words was getting undue attention. In the midst, I do as I always do, I keep my head down and did what I was there to do...teach.

THE STORY

As I guided my students through a phonetic lesson, little did I know that our routine would soon be disrupted by an unforeseen event that would redefine my role as a teacher and set me on a path toward a profound transformation.

This class lesson started like any normal lesson would....

"Open and closed syllables are important to decoding a word. Open syllables are going to make long vowel sounds, and closed syllables will make short vowel sounds. We practiced this yesterday, so today, we are going to do some syllabication. Take out your whiteboards and write the word *hello*."

The traumatic interruption begins:

"Hey, ya'll!" A six-year-old burst into our classroom, his innocent face shadowed by surprise and fear. A hushed tension blanketed the room as my small group of students exchanged horrified looks. This unexpected turn of events launched me into a high-stakes chase through the school halls. I was running in pursuit of a first-grade student with a potentially dangerous secret hidden in his backpack. No one knew this had happened, and I didn't know what would happen next, so the urgency of the situation echoed in my head. I chased him down the hallway, around corners, downstairs, and into the busy lunchroom filled with oblivious third, fourth, and fifth graders.

While I was in the middle of my reading lesson for my small group special education class, we were surprisingly interrupted by a young boy who flashed his book bag open and revealed to us a gun. At that moment, my mind starts to rush, and I see images of the countless school shootings that have rummaged through our nation. Although I was fully aware that a school shooting could happen in our school, however I was committed to protecting my classroom of scared children and a building full

27

of teachers and students who had no idea what I had just witnessed. With my military background and strong-minded personality, I had no choice but to jump into action to ensure the safety of every adult and child in the building. Now faced with a child contemplating his escape, I found myself grappling not only with the immediate danger but also with the challenge of discreetly alerting other teachers—a task that I never knew could be so hard.

In a tense situation, telling the cafeteria staff to safely deal with a student carrying a gun without alarming everyone was very tough. So I quickly went to the middle of the cafeteria and signaled to the other teachers that I needed help with this student. Together, in a very tense moment, we managed to safely escort the student to the office, finding a gun hidden in his backpack.

When my principal finally got word of what was happening, he was up in arms. But not for the reasons you may be thinking, but for the very opposite of what was needed at that moment. The principal and our governing body did everything they could to ensure that this situation stayed out of the community's ears, out of the news, and any other public outlet that would bring negative attention. In talking to the student and his parents on the day of the incident, it was clear to anybody with a heart and a mind of compassion that this student was crying out for help. Instead of answering the cry, they retreated because they feared who may be on the receiving end. In the aftermath, I'm left pondering the priorities of a school administration that says they care about kids but are more concerned with avoiding negative publicity than addressing the emotional needs of a troubled child.

Exploring the idea of transitioning from teaching to starting my venture

But on this one particular day, an unexpected turn of events shifts my life's purpose into drive. I was in complete dismay as to how they managed this situation. This student received a punishment as they should have, but that was it. Ronnie was a six-year-old who could not read, could not write, and could barely count to 100. I worked with this student day in and day out repetitively on the same academic concepts. We would try every way for the information to stick in his brain, but it didn't, and it's not that he couldn't. There were just so many other emotional and social factors that set a wall to his learning and that affected him each and every day. This was shown clearly through his misbehavior, which we dealt with on a daily basis. But Ronnie said on this particular day that we were not listening to him, so he felt as though this was his outlet, whether right or wrong, to make us listen, and we still didn't.

What they did at the school and as an organization built around the turnaround school model was place the school system's priorities above the needs of a child. The ins and outs and countless conversations of that particular day are somewhat of a blur to me, but what I do remember are the whispers across the school from many teachers of how they were glad I was the one to encounter the situation; they were glad that I was the one who had the training to defuse the situation. No one from the administration down to the janitor took the time to talk to me about my personal well-being and my social and emotional health after such a traumatic experience, or even ask why I think it happened. Everyone thanked me for a job well done and kept moving throughout their day as if nothing had happened.

I had tears on that day, not for myself but for something bigger than me: a broken educational system. I thought I had signed up to work in the educational system that would bring revolutionary change to a broken community. In actuality, I worked in an educational system that did not care about kids or their teachers. I worked in an educational system that thought a couple of days of suspension for a student with a gun and then back to the normal routine would solve the problems of a greater emotional need.

Days went by before my principal talked to me about what had happened that day. I am not sure if it was his inability to know how to connect with me and what to say or just a genuine disregard for my well-being, but either way, I did not know what I would do to make it through the school year under an administration that would treat us like this. As my God would have it, I was called to military duty for a few months right after this incident. It was a much-needed relief from the pressures of being at school every day, but the military would not last the entire year. By the time my orders were complete, I had four months left in the school year.

I had the option to quit or stick it out for the rest of the year. I was not raised to be a quitter, so I stuck it out to the end, but each day came with tears and steadfast prayers each morning on my long drive to school. Each morning, I felt like a ton of bricks was placed on my back, and the pressure from it was killing me. It was killing my drive and my purpose to educate kids. I had to come up with a plan and quickly.

I went home one day and told my husband I would be resigning at the end of the year and starting a tutoring center. I did not know what he would say, but being the loving and supportive husband that he is, he gave me his blessing. Months prior, I had been laying the groundwork by offering tutoring services after school, building a clientele, and preparing for a shift toward a more personalized educational journey. Several years earlier, I was captivated by the impact of Orton-Gillingham (OG) training on students with moderate intellectual disabilities. My administrators had chosen me to attend this training, and I had no idea what it was about. To my surprise, I loved every aspect of the concept we were taught, and I immediately implemented it in my classroom.

I did some research on advanced Orton-Gillingham training and discovered one of the top-rated Dyslexia schools in Atlanta. Intrigued, I invested in a year-long training at the Schenck School, delving deeper into the intricacies of Dyslexia. Witnessing how Dyslexia shaped a student's perspective of written language was eye-opening. I became increasingly excited about wielding the tools to unlock reading for underperforming students who struggled, not due to lack of effort but because they couldn't read. I immediately started working on my business plan to have the tutoring center up and running by the time the following school year started. I put it in my notice to let the school know I would not be returning the following school year. This intent was met with what I felt was an insincere request for me to stay because I was doing "great work." When I declined to stay, they thought it was worth mentioning that I would have to pay back a portion of my sign-on bonus. I kindly let them know that no money in the world was worth diminishing the purpose that God put on my life to ensure a holistic educational deposit was made into the lives of the students I teach.

In my opinion, for all students, but in this case, particularly our black students, it was important that the consequences were culturally responsive and had a sensitive approach. I say this not to be biased and accepting of the action because of his race but to ensure that strategies are equitable, fair, and tailored to meet the diverse needs of all students while being mindful of the cultural and societal contexts that may influence behavior. This is especially true because of the lower socioeconomic neighborhood that we worked in. Yes, there should have been a reprimand of some sort, but that reprimand was not followed up by anything that would target that student's social and emotional growth to ensure that this never happened again.

In my opinion, there are so many things that could have been done, such as taking this as a time to build a strong relationship between the student and the family beyond the academic performance so that there was a "village" mindset when having to interact with him for positive or negative behavior, come up with a positive reinforcement system that not always focused on his academic or behavioral weaknesses, collaborating with school counselors, social workers, and psychologist, or making this a chance for teachers and staff to reflect on their own practices, biases, and attitudes when it came to the population of students that we served. This incident becomes a turning point—a catalyst for me to reevaluate the purpose of education and the systems in place.

The final day of the school year, a day typically filled with the ritual of stacking chairs, dismantling bulletin boards, and hoping to return to the same classroom the next year, was different. This year marked the end of my tenure within the public school system. As I packed boxes, I felt a tinge of nostalgia, a bittersweet farewell to an era I had devoted my career to. Yet, beneath the surface lay a vision, a plan, and an unwavering faith that I was embarking on the right path. As I loaded those boxes into my car, I knew this moment was destined. With a vision crystallizing in my mind, I left the school that day, not just with the weight of packed boxes but with the lightness of purpose.

Reader Reflection

1. Personal Connection

   - What resonated most with you in this chapter?

   - What would you have done in this situation?

   - Have you experienced an educational moment that compelled you to rethink your path?

2. Challenges and Change

   - What challenges have you faced that have sparked a desire for change in your education or your child's education?

   - Reflect on a time when you had to act swiftly and decisively, as the author did in the cafeteria scene. What did you learn about yourself?

3. Growth and Adaptability
   - How do you relate to the author's struggle with adaptability when faced with unexpected challenges?
   - What steps have you taken to grow or adapt in your personal or professional life?

4. Looking Ahead
   - What changes do you hope to see or make in your own educational environment?

Chapter 2:
Venturing into
Entrepreneurship

The initial steps, challenges, and triumphs of stepping into the world of teacherpreneurship

The financial burden of starting a business with my own money was indeed overwhelming, particularly given the uncertainty of entrepreneurship. When I founded TREAD Educational Services, I decided to invest my teacher's retirement savings into the startup. I was also aware of the struggles small black businesses have with obtaining financial backing to start or sustain their businesses, and I felt like I didn't have any time to waste in search of that. I have heard the slogan "Don't use your own money to fund a business," and I am cognizant of that now, but at that time, I was eager to get started working in my purpose. This choice underscored the personal sacrifice and risk inherent in pursuing a business venture. It was a leap of faith, motivated by my deep passion for education and my desire to positively impact the lives of students.

I opened TREAD Educational Services, a tutoring center, in July 2018. TREAD is an acronym that stands for Teach Reach, Educate, Achieve, and DREAM. Our motto, "A Path to Success," encapsulated our mission to TEACH students to REACH academic success through individual EDUCATIONAL experiences that ultimately lead them to ACHIEVE their DREAMS. We offered a variety of services, including homework help, test prep, and remediation for academic deficits, but our specialty area was

Dyslexia and using Orton-Gillingham's multi-sensory reading method to teach students to read. That was our biggest seller. The demand for tutors with Dyslexia training was overwhelming and more than I could handle.

You see, that summer, a colleague connected me to a Special Education Coordinator from a county where they used to work. They were looking for a part-time lead special education teacher. I went for the interview for several reasons: 1) I was concerned about my financial security, not having navigated the business world before; 2) It was an administrator position, so I knew I would just be doing paperwork like IEPs, which I was good at, 3) I could make my own schedule, 4) It gave me financial security. Yes, I know #4 is repeated. This was a huge concern for me. Even with my husband's income and stepping out on Faith with the vision God gave me, I still wasn't confident in the success of it.

The interview went well, but I wasn't confident I would get the job. Three days later, I received a call offering me the position, which I accepted. Balancing the part-time administrative role with TREAD's demands proved challenging yet manageable during the first year. My schedule allowed me to continue tutoring in the evenings, creating a harmonious intersection of both worlds.

During the course of tutoring, I had a parent who had continually asked me to provide homeschool services to their child, but I declined because I knew that it wouldn't be financially worth it. I would have to quit my part-time position to do this. This parent was persistent and persuasive. As the spring of 2019 unfolded, I found myself in a meeting discussing the imminent launch of a school. Seven families were eager to enroll their children in a homeschool-modeled setting, even though it didn't align precisely with my initial vision. Many of the families didn't have significant reading issues, and the academic deficits were not extensive enough to warrant individualized education. Questions lingered: How did this align with my original vision? How would it sustain itself? Who was the target audience? Despite the uncertainties, the school was taking shape, birthing a chapter that would unfold with unexpected twists and turns.

August 2019 marked the beginning of TREAD Academy's second year, and it came with an unexpected twist—I was six months pregnant. The pregnancy, far from easy, demanded two instances of bed rest by the time I reached the halfway point. Transitioning from the structured routine of a normal school day to the irregular hours that entrepreneurship demanded took a toll on me physically, mentally, and emotionally. This exhaustion was different from what I experienced in my last year of teaching. This exhaustion was embraced with the joys of knowing I would be birthing life into my own child (something that I have always dreamed of and that doctors weren't sure would be possible). It was also the joy of bringing back hope to many students that education could be fun and they could learn.

Needless to say, with doors opening in August 2019, seven eager students entered, and the journey of TREAD Academy commenced. The initial phase went well; some aspects were in place, while others were similar to building a plane while flying it. A school counselor delved into the emotions of the students, a French teacher added a cultural flair, and a supportive group of parents stood ready to assist at a moment's notice. The curriculum, while not perfect, served its purpose as I, essentially a one-woman show, navigated the administrative side of the business. I didn't have a team of people who were helping with paperwork, accounting, lesson plans, and planning field trips. I had to make this all happen by myself. The complexities increased when I factored in my part-time administrative role.

Determined to make it work, I returned to my part-time position, hiring a parent from the school as my assistant on the days I couldn't be there. The juggling act unfolded seamlessly for three weeks, and I began to entertain the idea that maybe I was cut out for the world of entrepreneurship. Thoughts of scaling this model danced in my mind as I orchestrated plans for the remainder of the school year.

Amidst this, another memorable event loomed on the horizon—the baby shower scheduled for Labor Day weekend. At seven months pregnant, I was swollen, gaining water weight, and experiencing discomfort. I told the doctor about it, but they weren't concerned, so I continued living normally. A trip to the emergency room a few days before the baby shower revealed only Braxton Hicks contractions; I was released from the hospital and told to just rest. I forged ahead with the celebration, surrounded by love and support. The baby shower went off well, and we had a great time celebrating our soon-to-be bundle of joy.

The following day was Labor Day. My husband and I saw off our family that had come into town to celebrate with us, and then we spent the afternoon unwrapping gifts and making space for things we had no idea where to put. As the day went on, I started to feel more "off." I don't know exactly how to explain the pain that was in my body, but I just know it didn't feel right. My husband asked if I wanted to go to the hospital, but I declined, and he instead rang the on-call doctor to let them know about my symptoms. She instructed me to go to the hospital if I felt worse. I sat in the same spot on the couch all day, tossing and turning, hoping for some relief. That evening, I told my husband I would take a bath, and it would make me feel better. So, I did. I took a long, relaxing bath and started feeling revived. When I stood up and got out of the tub, all of the discomfort I felt all day came rushing back to me at once. I fell to my knees and crawled to the bedroom with just enough strength to call my husband, who was downstairs, and let him know I needed to go to the hospital. He came rushing and asked if we should pack a bag, and I said, "No, I want to get checked out and get back home to get some rest."

Within the next 30 minutes, we arrived at the emergency room. By the time we reached it, I was unable to stand on my own, and the world was spinning in uncontrollable circles. My husband carried me in and found me a wheelchair to sit in. I was aggravated because the front desk asked me questions I was too incoherent to answer. Nurses came and took my weight and blood pressure. Both were abnormally high. As I lay in bed crying in pain, hoping for answers, I am hooked up to so many monitors, none of which are giving positive readings. My husband was searching for answers, but no one could give him concrete updates. I knew things were taking a turn for the worse when they brought me a pill to take for my blood pressure. I am not the best at swallowing pills, which I let them know. They responded with these exact words: "Take this pill or die." They didn't need to say more. I figured out a way to swallow it.

Subsequent events unfolded rapidly. The urgency of an emergency C-section was declared, leaving my husband with the chilling revelation that they had to choose whom to save—me or our unborn child. Awakening from surgery, I grasped fragments of a reality that felt like a nightmare. My daughter was born, not breathing, resuscitated by the NICU team. Born eight weeks premature, she required an extended stay in the NICU. Meanwhile, my health was a precarious puzzle—preeclampsia, a severe onset, held me captive in the hospital. My blood pressure and iron levels refused to be tamed. The diagnosis of preeclampsia threw a wrench into the gears of my entrepreneurial journey. The focus shifted from the formation and continued success of TREAD Academy to an all-encompassing battle for my family's well-being and my own health. Yet, as I grappled with the challenges, the support from the remarkable group of parents surrounding me proved to be an unexpected anchor. They seamlessly took turns overseeing the students, ensuring that the learning journey continued, undisturbed by the unforeseen twists life had dealt us.

This chapter became not just a testament to a business's resilience but an emotional saga of survival, strength, and the unforeseen trials of entrepreneurship intertwined with the complexities of life. This would continue for two months straight. I would eventually return to work a few days a week because I was just sitting at home anxiously awaiting when our daughter would be released from the NICU. The school would keep my mind occupied.

Things took a somber turn, and the weight of the situation pressed upon me. My daughter's prolonged stay in the hospital demanded my attention and care, leaving me torn between her well-being, the emerging business, and the responsibilities of an unexpected pregnancy. Yet, with prayer and the dedication of the medical team, my daughter made her way out of the NICU into the warmth of home, and life started to regain a semblance of normalcy. The spark of joy from entrepreneurship rekindled as I pondered the possibility of this new venture becoming a legacy for my newborn daughter.

As the school days unfolded, the students indulged in a scrumptious Thanksgiving feast, reveled in a memorable holiday presentation, and shared laughter during conversations upon returning from the holiday break. January promised exciting field experiences, taking learning beyond the classroom walls, and the students embraced the idea wholeheartedly.

The unique challenges faced when transforming education amid a pandemic

However, just as the rhythm of our days seemed set, a new twist awaited. On the military side of things, I had applied for a First Sergeant position to which I was offered the job, a career development I was enthusiastic about. The start date at my new unit was a little unknown due to my unexpected pregnancy situation, but as things would have it, I began in January. Little did I know that the training schedule would soon alter my plans. I did not know that the training required for the position would have me gone so soon. Despite the initial shock, I held confidence in the capable parents who had proven their dedication earlier in the school year.

As March approached, I diligently prepared a comprehensive list of academic and social activities for the kids, aiming to avoid the last-minute chaos that ensued during my absence in September. Leaving the school on the last Friday of February, hope filled my heart for the upcoming month and excitement for my return in April.

Upon reaching the training venue, a bizarre narrative unfolded. The instructor shared a chilling story of his previous class graduating via Zoom due to many falling ill. The conversation revolved around COVID-19, a topic that had been making rounds on social media and the news. But the conversation surrounding it was nothing that I particularly felt was of concern. I did not for one second think that this would be a disease so deadly it would cause businesses to close their doors and for some-- permanently. Little did I anticipate that this virus would evolve into a global pandemic, altering the course of not just my life but countless others.

The initial weeks of training went by normally, with occasional jokes about a classmate potentially having "the Rona." It seemed like an inconvenience rather than a grave concern.

However, as the days passed and news of the virus's spread intensified, the atmosphere in the class shifted from casual banter to serious discussions and growing concerns. Who could ever imagine a place like the United States of America with no cars on the road, no people in the stores, no children in the schools, and no one going into the office? These were conversations that would become a reality.

To my surprise, within a span of 48 hours, our class was cut short, we graduated, and we were sent back to our respective homes. COVID-19 had become an imminent threat, disrupting plans and casting uncertainty over my newfound military endeavor. Anticipating my return to a buzzing school full of eager learners, I instead witnessed the closure of TREAD Academy's doors, mirroring the fate of countless businesses across the United States. The dream of an uninterrupted journey from tutoring to running a school now faced an unforeseeable hiatus. Sitting at home with my husband and newborn, we watched the news with a mix of disbelief and longing for a return to normalcy. From tutoring to a school, then pregnancy complications, a call to military duty, and now a worldwide pandemic, the challenges seemed insurmountable. The question lingered: How was I to sustain myself after such monumental events disrupted the carefully laid plans and my venture into entrepreneurship?

Reflecting on how my teaching experiences shaped the approach to entrepreneurship

As the dust of unforeseen challenges settled, I found myself standing at the precipice of the story of my professional journey. Navigating the business landscape, once a promising voyage, now demanded resilience and adaptability. In public schools, educational models transformed from physical to virtual spaces, a transformation driven by necessity yet rich with innovation. The challenge was not simply to replicate the classroom environment but to enhance it, leveraging technology to foster engagement, collaboration, and individualized learning experiences in ways that a physical classroom could not always accommodate.

The victories were many: students who thrived in the new digital realm, the creation of global classrooms without borders, and the democracy of education. We experimented with asynchronous learning platforms to cater to different time zones, incorporated multimedia resources to enrich the curriculum and employed virtual reality to bring abstract concepts to life. These initiatives required educators to become tech-savvy facilitators and students to be active participants in their learning journey. Yet, with triumphs came trials: the digital divide that disadvantaged some students, the struggle to maintain student engagement without physical presence, and the challenge of evaluating academic integrity. In response, they developed comprehensive support systems, including tech training for teachers, equipment lending programs for students, and innovative assessment methods focused on understanding over memorization. Public schools have been forced to create a way for the future of learning not to be confined to four walls, and they have done this through technology and virtual learning. Even with all the innovations, this abrupt change to the public school learning model still did not meet the needs of some students; it was not able to capture the learning style of all students. I was determined to provide an educational model (in-person) that took learning out of the four walls, textbooks, and repetitive sequence. Our learning would be an expansive, boundaryless, and personalized journey.

As I immersed myself in the realm of strategic planning, the demands of education persisted. Thus, I seamlessly transitioned into the virtual sphere of teaching, much like countless educators across America. What set my experience apart was the unique challenge of instructing multiple grade levels, spanning every subject, and engaging in one-on-one lessons throughout an extended school day. It was a struggle, and I needed to restructure what was happening and ensure continued success. The temporary closure of the school was not the end. I just knew that with some evaluation, strategizing, and rebuilding, an even better business plan would evolve than what I started with. I would evaluate the complexities of resurrecting a dream from the ashes, examining what elements of the initial vision were salvageable and what needed recalibration. The biggest aspect to tackle at this point in the journey was allowing myself to know and understand that the physical closure of the school did not mean the end of educational services and the transformative path forward that I was trying to create. Even though I was not busy savvy, I am very knowledgeable about the needs of students, and I just needed to ensure that I met the needs of students and then rebuild the business around that.

The closure of the physical school had profound implications for the financial landscape of the school. I was a new business owner. I took my teacher's retirement and invested it in the start-up of the business. We were used to a two-person income household. We just had a baby, and the bills didn't stop just because we were at home. This delicate dance of managing finances during turbulent times and exploring avenues for financial support and stability quickly taught me that if I continued this journey to transforming education, I would need multiple incomes to sustain myself. Amidst the chaos, community engagement emerges as a beacon of hope. The role of the community truly showed up in sustaining the educational vision. My parents agreed to pay partial tuition for online lessons, the students were fully engaged, and my landlords allowed me to skip a few months of rent. Through all the challenges that were faced over those six months, the nature of education took center stage.

The closure of the school prompted the evaluation of educational methodologies. What

I could not see in the midst of the storm was that this turmoil was a must in order to set sail on the path to education evolution. This journey was not my chosen path but a path pushed upon the narrative.

The classroom taught me empathy and developed my ability to listen and adapt to diverse needs, which became foundational in my business dealings. Every lesson plan, tailored to accommodate different learning styles, informed my approach to product development, ensuring that my services catered to a varied audience. Conflict resolution with students and parents improved my negotiation skills, which are vital for business partnerships and customer service. Likewise, the creativity and innovation required to engage students became a driving force in my entrepreneurial ventures, pushing me to think outside the box and develop unique educational solutions.

Reader Reflection

1. Relating to the Journey:
   - Reflect on a time when you took a significant risk, like starting a new venture. What motivated you, and how did it align with your personal values and goals?

2. Triumphs Along the Way:
   - Can you think of a moment of triumph in your life that came after overcoming a difficult challenge? How did you celebrate or acknowledge this success?

3. Transforming Education:
   - In what ways do you believe education needs to evolve to

better serve future generations? How can your experiences inform this evolution?

Chapter 3:
The Evolution of a
Teacherpreneur

Reflecting on personal growth, skill development, and evolution of my entrepreneurial identity

tanding at the crossroads of my life as a teacher and the world of business, I took a moment to think back. I saw how every lesson I taught and every challenge I faced in the classroom helped shape my plans for a new kind of school after the pandemic. It was like those classroom experiences were threads I used to weave a new kind of learning space that didn't follow the usual rules.

I think about the kids, each so different, with their own hurdles and hopes. Reaching each of them in their own way was the puzzle that made teaching both thrilling and daunting. Those moments were when they figured out how to connect and make the material come alive for them—that was the spark. It was the kind of spark that doesn't just fade away; it kindles a flame, a burning desire to do more, to be more.

When the pandemic hit the world, and our classrooms went from blackboards and laughter to pixels and silence, I felt lost at sea. But it was in that uncertainty, in the challenge of teaching through a screen to faces I could no longer see, that a new path revealed itself. I embraced the chaos, finding in it the seeds of a new beginning. I began to weave these threads into a vision—a school without walls, a space where learning was as boundless as the imagination and as personal as each student's dream. Creating this non-traditional learning environment wasn't just about bucking the system or breaking rules. It was about constructing a shelter where education could thrive unfettered by one-size-fits-all lessons, where every child's needs weren't just met but anticipated and celebrated.

Venturing into the world of teacher entrepreneurship was nothing shy of scary. As I previously insinuated, business management was not my field of expertise. I studied education, knew education, and I loved teaching. I felt like and continue to feel like I know what's best for students and don't want the constraints of someone telling me how to do it. I know how to provide an educational space that is dedicated to the success of every individual need and any student that docks our doorway. I didn't know at the time, and what I am continuing to learn is the business aspect of being a teacher entrepreneur.

Highlighting specific challenges faced and the strategies employed to overcome them.

Being a business owner comes with its share of harsh truths. Contrary to the glamorous image portrayed, the reality is far from it. As the owner, I've experienced the daunting responsibility of being the last to receive payment, often sacrificing personal financial stability for the sake of the business. Additionally, I find myself consistently being the first one to arrive at work and the last one to leave, juggling numerous responsibilities along the way. What's more, when things inevitably go sideways, I bear the brunt of the blame, with little recognition for the hard work and dedication poured into the venture. It's a lonely journey at times, characterized by uncertainty and relentless pressure. Despite the challenges, I continue to persevere, fueled by a deep passion for what I do and a commitment to seeing my vision come to fruition.

You know, people always say that you are never really successful in the business world until you are working on your business and not in your business. I do believe that statement to be true, but it has been and continues to be a struggle to remove myself from the classroom and the teaching because that's what I'm passionate about but as a business owner, you also understand that there is a point at which it becomes very overwhelming to do the work and to build. As I write this book, I find myself in the throes of building a ship while navigating treacherous waters, yet I have no fear, for the ship remains afloat. We've weathered a few storms and faced some choppy seas, but ultimately, we continue to reach safe shores with each day's journey. When you take that leap of faith and jump into the work that we are doing, it is by far anything easy; it is by far anything that would sustain you financially, at least in the beginning. It is by far anything for the weak of heart. When you commit to this work, you commit to early mornings and late evenings, lifelong learning, going above and beyond for every student, and a by-any-means necessary attitude to ensure a student's mastery of skills.

Among all these commitments, I am still a mother, a wife, a daughter, a sister, a cousin, a niece, a friend, a military member, a church member, and I have to remember self-care. Considering all of these roles that I play, how do I give 100% to each area of my life as I attempt to bring reformation to an area of our society that has been status quo for hundreds of years? This work is going to be an uphill battle that requires all of my attention, and the honest answer, as I'm sure you figured out by now, is that I absolutely cannot give 100% to everything. Each day brings something a little different, and on the easier days, I can devote myself more to home, and on the harder days, I devote myself more to overcoming that entrepreneurial challenge. There is some area in your life that is going to lack when you set forth on this journey. My success has come because of my faith in God and the support that I have from my husband, my daughter, my family, my friends, and the community around me that believes in what I'm doing.

As you read this book and if you believe that this is the work that you should be doing, I urge you to have a community of people who support you and believe in the work that you are doing. One of my toughest battles has always been handing over the reins to those around me—whether it's a family member stepping in, a teacher on my team, or a volunteer from our community.

I've grappled with the notion that if I want something done right, I should do it myself instead of spending precious time coaching someone else to meet my high standards. However, here's the raw truth I've faced in my entrepreneurial journey: to truly rise, you need to lift others alongside you. Empowering the people who've got your back means they can help carry the load, making it a bit lighter for everyone. Anyone who knows me knows that I've often longed for a way to directly transfer all my plans and visions into the minds of my staff and supporters, bypassing endless explanations.

However, the reality is starkly different. So now, atop my ever-growing to-do list, I pencil in time for training, mentoring, and coaching. It's about investing in those who walk this path with me for our students' success and our educational mission's future.

I'm one of the few schools in my area that employs several teachers, which I call learning facilitators. I believe in our model of small group and one-on-one learning time. Since our school is tuition-based, employing several people to take on this task is not an easy financial decision because I'm not profiting enough to afford multiple teachers. I have been fortunate enough to retain learning facilitators who believe in the path we are taking to reach kids.

One strategy that I have employed is looking for college education majors and retired teachers because they have more financial flexibility to journey with us as we build up to sustainability. My end goal is not to become a millionaire from what I'm doing. My goal is to ensure by any means necessary the success of every student that attends TREAD Academy.

I often use this statement: "The school is my passion and not my paycheck." I had to make the conscious decision not to pay myself when this all started to ensure that my overhead cost and payroll were taken care of every month. When I tell people this, I get all kinds of crazy looks, side eyes, and eyebrows raised. Even my husband questioned my decision to do that, but being the loving, caring, and supportive husband that he is, he understood my decision. We are growing towards sustainability, so things look different for us financially now, but only because I gave myself the grace and patience to grow.

I work a part-time job to help build my multi-streams of income. The work is still in the field of education, so it does not burden me to do it. Many other microschool leaders will tell you the same thing. Being completely dependent on these models of education as your sole income (initially) is not the smartest move. We were at an event one time, and parents were coming over to learn more about the school and the model that we have created for students and I had one particular individual come over, and I asked them what information they would like to know about our school and how I could be of service to their child. They didn't have many questions about servicing their child but more about how the school was set up and how I got started.

As we engaged in conversation for a few minutes, the last question that she asked me was, "How profitable is your school?"

I guess she could tell from the look on my face that I was puzzled by the question because it was my assumption that I was talking to a potential parent. She then went on to tell me that she was a teacher, and she only came to the event to learn more about our schools and how we were doing things, and the potential for her to come out of the public school system and do the same. I am absolutely on board with helping any teacher who wants to come out of the classroom and do the work that we are doing, especially black educators. That is one of my main purposes in writing this book. However, I am not okay with any teacher who comes out of the classroom thinking that this is going to be a get-rich-quick scheme.

We live in this microwave attitude generation. They believe that everything should happen fast and will invest in anything with six and seven-figure potential. I don't blame them because the cost of living in America is not getting any cheaper, but I'm here to tell you that in the world of teacher entrepreneurship and the work that we do, you are setting yourself up for failure by thinking that you are going to open a school and make a lot of money. I'm not telling you not to pay yourself because that is unrealistic, though I am telling you to give yourself grace and the patience to grow into financial stability.

If you are in this for the money, it is in your best interest to stay where you are and continue to do what you are doing. The evolution of teacher entrepreneurs is not an overnight success story. This is also not to say that you couldn't potentially be very financially successful with it, but if that's your focus, you will lose sight of the sure prize, which is the student. Traditional school settings view students as numbers, and every seat is a dollar amount. It's as if the student is just another transaction. Those of us who are building non-traditional settings are looking for transformational learning, not transactional learning.

Specific data regarding the closure rate of microschools due to financial issues is not readily available, being a relatively new and diverse educational phenomenon. There is no comprehensive and centralized reporting on their reasons for closure, but I personally know a few that have closed and others who may close. Where does this leave our black students from underserved communities? They end up back in the same educational box we tried to pull them out of. For this educational reform, we are looking for individuals who have patience and long-term sustainable ideas so that we don't open up our doors for two years to then close and fail our children.

At the close of this book, my story will still continue, and I know that in the near future, I will be able to say that I am financially successful and the school is financially sustainable, but I am not knocking down every door and sending every email with the intention of financial gain. I do not expect you to understand, grasp, and be content with this idea right now because it took me a while to come to grips with it.

As you may remember from Chapter 2, I did not want to start the homeschool group that parents asked for because it did not make financial sense to me. The more I heard their story and the more I heard the cry for help; I chose to rearrange my life for the betterment of their children and for the betterment of my future children. I had a calling on my life and could not decide to ignore that calling because of what the money looked like. As I continue to do this work, I believe that it will all come back to me 10 times over, and I am thankful for it in advance. I do not expect you to rearrange your life, but I ask that you evaluate the possibility of this educational reformation being a part of your journey.

On the business side of things, I've had to learn to deal with payroll companies, the IRS system, bookkeeping, finding commercial space, interviewing, creating social media platforms, creating email lists, opening business bank accounts, applying for grants and loans, marketing and the list goes on and on and on.

When you think of everything that needs to be done for your business to succeed, I again ask you, how do I give 100% to the business and everything else? It will be a give-and-take approach, but you won't despise this idea if you're called to do this work.

I am no expert at what it takes to build a business, grow a business, and sustain a business, but I do believe that I have had the experiences, the successes, the failures, the conversations, and the positive and negative encounters that will help the teachers coming behind us, wanting to join in our educational reform. I believe that I've learned well enough in all the business aspects to help a teacher set up a school geared towards humble beginnings and successful continuation. My evolution into a teacher entrepreneur has been successful. Some may feel otherwise, but in that case, we now have to evaluate one person's meaning of success compared to another person's perspective on success. Success here is the happiness, the growth, the ability to dream and succeed beyond their wildest measures, and the academic experiences our students are exposed to daily.

As I don the many hats of an entrepreneur, I often pause to reflect on the growth that's taken place. Each challenge has expanded my horizons, and with every step forward, I carry the lessons of the classroom with me, the heart of a teacher still beating strong beneath the mantle of a business owner.

Reader Reflection

1. Reflect on a moment in your own life or teaching career where you experienced significant personal growth. What catalyzed this change?

2. Can you identify a skill you've developed in recent years? How has this skill impacted your personal life in the classroom?

3. Entrepreneurship often requires a strong sense of self. How has your identity evolved with your professional experiences?

4. Think about a challenge you've faced that has shaped your approach to work or

leadership. How did overcoming this challenge change you?

5. How do you balance personal growth with professional demands, and what strategies do you use to ensure both are being addressed?

Chapter 4:
Beyond Borders:
Impact and Outreach

Strategies and insights into fostering partnerships and collaborations within the education business community.

D iving into the deep end, that's what it felt like when I first embarked on the journey to intertwine the threads of education with the fabric of our community. I was a teacher with a dream, a dream where learning broke free from the rigid confines of tradition and embraced each child's individual needs. It was a path less traveled, filled with the promise of innovation but punctured with the complications of change. My heart was set, and my goals were etched in my mind, yet finding the partners to join me in this educational revolution was like searching for a lighthouse in a foggy sea. In the early chapters of this adventure, my role wavered between that of an enthusiastic believer and a solitary activist. I saw potential where others saw risk; I envisioned transformation where others were content with the status quo. The local businesses, the non-profits, the leaders who held the keys to the community's heart—they were my audience, and I was a storyteller armed with nothing but a belief and a vision for a better future.

The journey towards sustainable community partnerships in the realm of non-traditional education was parallel to navigating uncharted waters. The struggle lay not in the lack of willingness but in the inherent challenge of making organizations aware of the pressing need for an alternative approach to education.

Conventional education held a steadfast position, and the need for an alternative was only sometimes apparent to those whose support was crucial. It was crucial to close the achievement gap between black students and their peers, to promote economic empowerment and social equity for the black community, and to promote diversity in education so that they could see themselves represented in the learning content and leaders. Convincing organizations of the urgency for change became a fascinating yet difficult narrative within the larger story.

Imagine feeling alone on this island of educational reformation and then being able to find a group of like-minded individuals who are in some sense pursuing your same passions and dreams, only to then enter into a realm of struggle, combativeness, jealousy, and overall crabs in a barrel mentality. During my time as a teacherpreneur, I have tried to join forces with many organizations and community partners who I felt were headed down the same narrow path I was; they were, but, in all actuality, their mindset did not align with my idea of what a safe, fun and productive educational environment looked like for children. Our mindsets also did not align with the "how" to get to the next level of our journey. You really can attribute it to the same idea of a school with many different classrooms and many different teachers. Each teacher walks into their classroom each day with the intent to fulfill the mission and vision of that particular school or school district, but in the reality of that classroom, everyone is operating in a way that they deem best or, should I say, to the best of their ability and potential.

In the same school building, there is chatter and gossip about what this teacher is doing, what that classroom is doing, and how one student is performing versus another student. There is gossip and chatter about who will be teacher of the year and if they truly deserve it. The same sentiments are happening out here in the world of micro-schools and teacher entrepreneurs who believe they have built an educational model that is best for children. Then down the street or in another city or in another state, you have another micro-school that believes they are doing what is best for children.

What I have discovered in my time as an edupreneur is that, we are all doing what is best for children in our own way, in our own space, and catering to the specific students that we serve. In my eyes, that is amazing work. That is work that deserves Teacher of the Year. No one person is lesser than, and no one person is greater because of the work that they are doing; everyone is doing work that is applicable to the population that they serve. It is unfortunate that in my teacherpreneur experience, I have run into countless roadblocks in trying to form communities and organizations of teachers of like minds (who know that the public school is not the way for students and have created a space that they think is great for students) because they can't move away from the crab in a barrel mentality and cheer for everyone's success. Everyone is still trying to prove to each other whose program is better, which is more successful, whose program gets the most spotlight, and whose program is the most sustainable. There is no time for this conversation in the realm of what we do. Every day is vital to ensuring the path to success is laid. The only way to succeed is to unite as a cohesive collective of like-minded individuals and serve children. The waters are rough, and the seas are too unknown for us to navigate this alone.

Microschools and nontraditional education are uncharted waters for educational reform. Education has gained such a political shape that our nation, as a whole, is scared to touch the reformation of education. Even dare to dream of what education in the 21st century should and could be—knowing that when you step out into the world of teaching, entrepreneurship, micro-schools, learning pods, and any other non-traditional setting, you're stepping out there on faith with just a dream, a vision, and a mission to do the best you can with what you have knowing that you don't have local status, state funding, or government support and recognition.

Microschools are like "Mom and Pop shops" or "Boutique hotels." It is my belief that we should be Marriotts and Four Seasons. So how do we gain that support and create that community of teachers who know this is a time for change in education? The only way we do that is by forming our own collectives, our own organizations, and our own community of leaders who know and understand what a safe space for underserved, underrepresented, and overlooked students in our community should look like. Whether that is a local organization or national organization, it is our duty to create and curate a sustainable and viable educational reform committee.

This process will and has involved meticulous storytelling—painting a vivid picture of the gaps in traditional education, showcasing the limitations faced by students, and explaining how a non-traditional approach could fill those gaps. This narrative was not just about an alternative but about nurturing a collective understanding that education is evolving and that our community is pivotal in steering this evolution.

Engaging with local businesses became a delicate task of articulating how investing in non-traditional education was an investment in the community's future workforce. The struggle was to secure financial backing and convey the symbiotic relationship between a well-educated, skilled workforce and a thriving local economy. Bridging this awareness gap required presentations and an ongoing dialogue acknowledging concerns and providing tangible solutions.

The initial challenge and continuous ongoing challenge of engaging with local businesses and community leaders is the need for knowledge behind this new way of education. As previously stated, as a nation, we are entrenched in the image of what education has been, which skews our ability to see what education could be. Many business owners and community leaders respond with the idea and the notion of giving the public school a chance. They urge parents to send their children to public schools because public schools have the resources to ensure their educational success. The parents who are seeking out alternative education already tried the traditional route. These leaders and business owners fail to understand that the public school is pumped with millions and millions of dollars every year and is still producing the same mediocre results.

Millions of children cannot read, write, or calculate the money in their bank account even though the government is pumping their schools with money for what they would consider a "good education." I am here to express to every leader, activist, business owner, public education leader, and political influencer the fact that we are not against public school by any means, but we understand that public school is not for every child or every teacher. We have an understanding that public schools cannot successfully and effectively reach every student.

I have student testimonials of how, since our school started, they feel more confident in class because of the focus more on individual learning styles. They have also said that they were scared to ask questions, but now they feel like it's okay to be curious and even make mistakes. They have proclaimed that our teaching model cares about students and has drastically changed their lives. It is now my job as a teacher entrepreneur to empower parents to regain full control of their child's education. That does not mean they must come to my school or anyone else's learning spaces. It simply means that parents are more educated about the educational options that are now available to them without feeling stuck at their local public school. In doing this, parents are now having to (possibly) pay private tuition to microschools so that they can send their child off every morning with the confidence that they are coming back home having truly been cared for and having truly been educated in a manner that best meets their needs. This same parent also pays taxes to a local school district that cannot ensure their child's success. This can't be considered fair in the eyes of political leaders and policymakers, but, unfortunately, it is the way they operate.

Advocating for and contributing to the growth of non-traditional learning in the education and business landscape.

As part of our outreach to make a broader impact, our students, parents, and staff participate in advocacy at our local state government. As you will notice towards the end of this book, the idea of advocating for political change is part of what students are actively doing through what we consider competency-based learning and field experiences. It is part of our living and learning model. Not only is it an educational moment for them, but it is also a real-life experience in which they can speak up and speak out to local representatives about how they feel about their education. This is something that many children do not get the opportunity to express. This is also an opportunity for parents and staff to speak with representatives from their perspectives on how educational reform impacts their lives and their households.

In the short year that we have participated in advocacy, I realized that the leaders and policymakers are so far removed from the decisions they are voting on that they have an ignorance towards our perspectives. We are the ones in the trenches every day. We are making do every day with our limited resources, truly reaching the whole child and meeting them at their point of need. However, we have heard leaders respond to us with demeaning undertones, letting us know that the spaces we have chosen to teach in and send our children to for education are personal choices and that is nothing state or government policy should have to participate in. We have also been told that simply parents are not smart enough to choose the right environment for their children. Hearing and experiencing all of this negativity towards educational reform leads me to stand and proclaim even harder the idea that we of like minds, must come together as one unified force and create our own seats and our tables and start our own discussion about what is right for students.

So, to say that our mission for a broader outreach has been a struggle is an understatement, but it is not unattainable. I have had success in building relationships and partnerships with local businesses. For example, we have partnered with a financial institution that houses the monies of our students as they learn to navigate financial literacy as part of one of our competency-based learning programs for our school. We have also successfully partnered with a local community center that provides the physical space for us to engage in activities, such as sports and social events we have for the school. We have also been successful in receiving small-scale donations from small businesses that read about our mission and vision and are willing to contribute, not in a financial way, but through a service that benefits school events. One partnership I am most proud of is the local small businesses that have committed to allowing my middle and high school students to do apprenticeship hours in their space and gain the skills and knowledge needed to be successful in their postsecondary education or the workforce.

Another idea to tackle as we aim for a broader outreach is to recognize that as teacher entrepreneurs, we are now also community leaders. As community leaders in the realm of education, our schools can build partnerships to champion educational innovation. What I am aware of is that as an individual, as a teacher, and as a business owner, I do not have all of the answers. I am also aware that joining forces with other community leaders will allow us to win this race and truly create a mind-blowing transformation in education. I have realized over the time that we have been operating that as we bring awareness to educational reform, that awareness has to turn into tangible support and action.

The community at large has to not just hear about what you're doing. They have to see and interact with what you are doing. As the saying goes, "I can show you better than I can tell you," in our world of educational reform, our students are our showcase. I urge any business or organization that is reading this to reach out and come see the amazing work that our students are doing; anyone who leaves our schools will be ready for whatever they decide to do post-secondary.

We will search high, and we will search low for the resources and support that the students need to be successful in any area they want to venture into, but I need you to know that this journey can be more impactful and more innovative with the support of local and national organizations, leaders, and politicians. The goal is to bring awareness and to mobilize the community's influential voices to amplify the urgency for change.

Reader Reflection

1. How did the testimonials in this chapter change or reinforce your perspective on the education system?

2. Have you observed or experienced the impact of educational disparities in your own community?

3. What do you believe are the most urgent changes needed in today's education system to support all students, and why?

4. How can communities unite to ensure educational reforms are inclusive and equitable?

5. If you were to create an educational program, what aspects would you focus on to support the needs of marginalized students?

6. What role can individuals play in advocating for improved educational opportunities for Black students?

CHAPTER 5:
Celebrating Success: Milestones And Achievements

Reflecting on Key Milestones

As I reflect on the journey from the inception of TREAD Educational Services to the flourishing establishment of TREAD Academy, I am filled with a profound sense of gratitude for the transformative milestones we have achieved. Each milestone represents not only a triumph in the realm of education but also a testament to our community's unwavering dedication and collaborative spirit. Transitioning from a modest tutoring center to a fully accredited school was a monumental step forward. It signified the evolution of our vision, from providing supplemental educational support to offering a comprehensive learning experience that nurtured the holistic development of our students. The journey was not without its challenges, but with perseverance and a shared commitment to excellence, we forged ahead, turning obstacles into opportunities for growth.

One of the most gratifying aspects of our journey has been the steady increase in enrollment year after year. This surge in student enrollment is not merely a numerical achievement; it reflects the trust and confidence that families place in our educational philosophy and approach. It validates the impact we are making in the lives of our students and their families, empowering them to dream big and pursue their aspirations with confidence.

Achieving accreditation was a pivotal moment in our trajectory. It was a recognition of the high standards of academic rigor, student support, and administrative excellence that we uphold at TREAD Academy. Accreditation opened doors to new opportunities for our students, from advanced placement programs to partnerships with colleges and universities, laying the groundwork for their future success.

Receiving our first grant was a significant milestone that fueled our mission to provide high-quality education to all students, regardless of their background or circumstances. The grant provided financial support and served as a vote of confidence in our innovative approach to education. It validated the impact we are making in the community and is a testament to the power of collaboration in driving positive change. One of the most heartening achievements has been the consistently high student return rate, with 95% of our students choosing to return to TREAD Academy year after year. This remarkable retention rate speaks volumes about the sense of belonging and community we have cultivated at our school. It is a testament to the strong relationships we have built with our students and their families and the unwavering support they have shown us throughout our journey.

Collaborative Success Stories

Our success at TREAD Academy is not solely attributed to our internal efforts but is deeply rooted in the collaborative partnerships we have forged with local businesses, parents, and the broader community. These partnerships have been instrumental in enriching the educational experience at our school and expanding our reach to a wider audience. Local businesses have played a vital role in supporting our mission through sponsorships, mentorship programs, and internship opportunities for our students. By opening their doors and sharing their expertise, these businesses have provided invaluable real-world experiences that have enriched our curriculum and prepared our students for success in the workforce. For example, a partnership with a local financial institution has allowed our students to learn about real-world financial readiness, savings, and investments, while a collaboration with a nearby farm has enabled hands-on lessons in agriculture and sustainability.

Parental involvement has been another cornerstone of our success. Parents have become equal partners in their children's educational journey through active participation in school activities, teaching classes in their area of expertise, volunteering, and feedback sessions. Their insights, support, and advocacy have been invaluable in shaping our programs and ensuring that we are meeting the diverse needs of our students. Our collaboration with the broader community has also been instrumental in driving positive change. From organizing community events to participating in outreach programs, we have worked hand in hand with community leaders and organizations to address pressing issues and create a more inclusive and equitable learning environment for all students.

You may be wondering why this chapter is shorter than the previous ones. Well, our story of how we began is past, but our journey to educational reform is far from over. We are five years into our non-traditional approach to education, and what we have done and seen so far is working. Many entrepreneurial endeavors fail within the first five years. Those who survive beyond five years typically do so by demonstrating resilience, strategic planning, and an ability to innovate continually. I am proud to celebrate even the smallest successes and milestones because any of the challenges we faced, in the beginning, could have been the end of my dream of a brighter future for kids. So, our story continues, and we prepare for the many more success stories and collaborations that will arise from the great work that we will do for years to come. As the great saying goes, "The best is yet to come!".

Reader Reflection

1. Looking at your own life, what lessons have you learned that could be valuable to someone starting their entrepreneurial journey into microschools? Look at this question from the perspective of a parent or a teacher.

CHAPTER 6:
Future Horizons:
What Lies Ahead

TREAD Goals

As I gaze towards the future horizons of TREAD Academy and my aspirations as a teacherpreneur, I am filled with a profound sense of purpose and determination. My vision extends far beyond the walls of our current microschool, encompassing a broader mission to normalize non-traditional education and school choice as viable pathways for students across the nation. One of my primary goals is to expand the reach of non-traditional education by opening more school locations across the country. By establishing additional microschools in black communities, we can provide students with access to innovative learning environments catering to their needs and aspirations. These new locations will serve as hubs of academic excellence and inspirations of educational innovation, inspiring other educators and communities to embrace alternative approaches to schooling.

Central to this vision is the creation of a replicable model of education that can be implemented in communities far and wide. It is essential to move beyond the limitations of the cookie-cutter education system and instead focus on building educational systems that prioritize the holistic development of each child. By developing a scalable model that emphasizes personalized learning pathways, student-centered instruction, and a focus on character development, we can empower educators and communities to reimagine the possibilities of education. By supporting non-traditional education and school choice, we can create a paradigm shift in how society views schooling. No longer should students be confined to a one-size-fits-all educational approach that fails to meet their diverse needs and aspirations. Instead, we must strive to build a future where every child has access to an educational experience that nurtures their unique talents, passions, and potential.

As I embark on this journey towards a future where non-traditional education is the norm rather than the exception, I am guided by an unwavering belief in the transformative power of education. Together, we can create a world where every child has the opportunity to thrive, succeed, and become the best version of themselves. The horizon is bright, and the possibilities are endless.

Developing An Ecosystem Of Non-Traditional Education

In order to build a sustainable model, we must be an ecosystem of educational environments and resources that support our approach to education. This ecosystem must start with a mindset shift and then an academic shift. Microschool education models are starting to see classroom instruction evolve to incorporate project-based and inquiry-based learning, diminishing the reliance on traditional rote memorization and standardized testing. We are at the point of seeing a more pronounced integration of adaptive learning technologies that tailor educational content to individual student needs, thereby making learning more personalized and efficient.

It is my hope that these changes will influence educational standards and practices, potentially leading to a more holistic and skills-based approach to education that equips students for the complexities of the modern world. The aim is to foster a system where student engagement exceeds passive learning, encouraging students to participate actively in their education through inquiry-based learning and real-world problem-solving.

It is essential to empower educators to be innovators and leaders. This can be achieved by providing professional development that not only updates their academic skills but also equips them with the tools to implement new teaching methods. Creating think tanks within educational organizations can foster a culture of innovation, where teachers can collaborate on developing new curriculum models and teaching strategies.

We must strive for truly inclusive systems where student backgrounds and learning needs are acknowledged, celebrated, and catered to. Such systems would dismantle one-size-fits-all approaches, instead offering multiple pathways to success that honor the variety of ways in which students learn and interact with the world. To ensure every voice contributes to this vision, we must implement opportunities that bring diverse stakeholders to the table—from students and parents to educators and policymakers. These opportunities should be designed to uplift marginalized voices and provide resources that lower the barriers to participation in our ecosystem.

Call To Action

To shape the future of education into a landscape that thrives on innovation and inclusivity, it's crucial for all stakeholders— educators, policymakers, parents, and students—to engage actively in its development. This engagement can include participating in educational forums, contributing to policy discussions, and providing feedback on curriculum developments. Policymakers can craft legislation that supports innovative educational models and ensures equitable access for all students. Parents and students can voice their needs and experiences, advocating for changes that reflect the diverse ways in which learners engage with information. Communities can unite to create educational initiatives that reflect their unique cultural and societal needs. Navigating education's unchartered territories and establishing an ecosystem starts with you!

Reader Reflection

1. How do you envision the future of education, and what role do you see yourself playing in it?

2. What emerging trends in education excite you the most, and why?

3. How can you, as an individual, contribute to the positive evolution of educational systems?

4. What steps can be taken to ensure that future educational initiatives are equitable and accessible to all learners?

5. How can educators, policymakers, parents, and students work together to

shape a future that values lifelong learning and adaptability?

Conclusion

Believing in myself when others didn't was both challenging and empowering. Despite facing skepticism and doubt from those around me, I remained steadfast in my conviction and vision. This unwavering self-belief became my driving force, propelling me forward even when the path seemed uncertain. Instead of letting others' opinions dictate my actions, I used their skepticism as fuel to prove them wrong. This journey taught me the importance of self-confidence and resilience in the face of adversity. While the road was often lonely and tense with obstacles, staying true to my beliefs ultimately led me to success. It reinforced the notion that self-trust is paramount in achieving one's goals, serving as a powerful reminder that sometimes, the only person you need to believe in you is yourself.

But beyond the individual journey lies a broader narrative—a narrative of hope, inspiration, and the enduring impact of education. As I celebrate the milestones and achievements recorded within these pages, I'm reminded of the profound influence that dedicated educators, innovative approaches, and supportive communities can have on shaping the future. In the face of adversity, this memoir is a testament to the strong spirit of those who dare to dream, refuse to settle for the status quo, and strive to make a meaningful difference in the world. It's a story of resilience in the face of challenges, perseverance in pursuing one's passions, and the transformative power of education to change lives.

As we stand at the precipice of tomorrow, looking out over the expansive horizon of educational possibilities, I am reminded of the profound journey that has brought me here. My path has been winding and uncertain. The future of education is not a distant dream but an unfolding reality that we are actively shaping with each passing moment. In this journey, we are not mere passengers but navigators, charting a course towards horizons that promise a better future for our kids and our communities. We should aspire to create learning environments that not only impart knowledge but also foster the kind of critical thinking and adaptability that will be essential in the rapidly changing landscapes of the future. We seek to empower today's learners and inspire tomorrow's educators, leaders, and innovators. The path ahead will require us to be bold, question the status quo, and embrace the unknown with an open mind and heart. It will call for collaboration across disciplines and cultures and a commitment to the kind of lifelong learning that extends beyond the classroom walls.

As I reflect on the progress I have made and other educational leaders around me, I also acknowledge the work that remains. We must ensure that education continues to be a beacon of hope and a catalyst for change. Let us then move forward with a sense of purpose and optimism, carrying with us the lessons of the past, the knowledge of the present, and the vision for a future where education is the foundation of a thriving and equitable society. This is our legacy and our promise—as educators, as learners, as a community—to the generations that will follow.

Work With US!

TREAD Academy is powered by our model of "Empowering Education and Advancing Dreams." The school model is built on a foundation of innovation, equity, and community engagement. It prioritizes data-driven decision-making, personalized learning, parental empowerment, and school autonomy to create a dynamic and student-centric educational environment. At the core of the model is a commitment to providing high-quality education that meets the diverse needs of students. This is achieved through personalized learning pathways tailored to individual student needs, supported by a robust student analytics performance portfolio platform that informs instructional practices and competency-based learning. The school fosters strong partnerships with local businesses, educational entities, and community organizations to ensure a collaborative approach to educational reform and advocacy for school choice. Through these partnerships, the school aims to expand access to high-quality education, particularly in underserved communities.

Furthermore, the school model emphasizes the importance of community involvement and parental engagement, providing resources and workshops to empower parents to make informed decisions about their children's education.

Interested in building a proven model? Visit my website for more information and to register for one-on-one sessions with me.

Coaching with me will give you a proven model to use with the autonomy to make it your own and focus on your niche.

www.denicedixon.com

Below is a summary of what your coaching sessions will cover:

Session 1: Understanding Microschools

Session 2: Planning Your Microschool

Session 3: Legal and Regulatory Considerations

Session 4: Curriculum and Teaching

Session 5: Enrollment and Marketing

Session 6: Operations and Administration

Session 7: Launching Your Microschool

Resource and References

Websites:

- www.treadacademy.com
- https://edupreneuracademy.org/

Courses:

- ASU Prep Microschool Entrepreneur Fellowship

Organizations:

- VELA Education Fund
- National Microschooling Center
- EdChoice
- Black Microschools ATL

About The Author

Denice S. Dixon is a dedicated educator, educational advocate, businesswoman, and member of the Air Force Reserves, with a proven record of leadership, planning, and educational excellence. With a Bachelor of Science in Elementary and Special Education from the University of North Carolina at Greensboro, Master of Education from American Military University, and Certification as an Orton-Gillingham specialist from Schenck School, Denice has consistently demonstrated expertise in the education realm, instruction strategies, and intervention that meets the needs of students.

DENICE DIXON

In 2018, Mrs. Dixon established TREAD Educational Services, LLC and 2019 TREAD Academy, Inc. which provides personalized tutoring and comprehensive non-traditional curriculum instruction to neurotypical and neurodivergent students in grades Pre-K to 12th grade. She also works as an education advocate with The Kline Firm and is highly knowledgeable and experienced in the field of special education and students with dyslexia. As a former public-school special education teacher and a special education administrator, she has worked in multiple districts in the state of Georgia.

Her well-rounded abilities to support classroom teachers, assess student performance, and ensure compliance with educational standards have allowed her to build an educational infrastructure that is positively impacting students. Whether in the classroom or in military service, Denice brings a commitment to excellence, a strategic approach to challenges, and a heart for service, making her an invaluable asset to the field of education and beyond.

www.ingramcontent.com/pod-product-compliance
Lightning Source LLC
Chambersburg PA
CBHW060539130626
46553CB00002B/818